MW00958952

Easter
Joke
Book

Who is the Easter Bunny's favorite actor?

Anthony HOPkins.

Why should Easter eggs beware of good jokes? They may crack up!

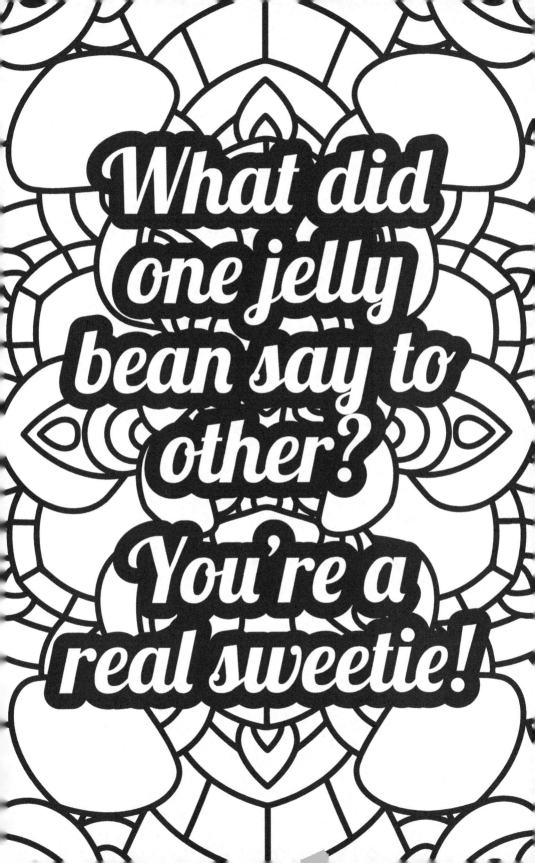

Who did the Easter Bunny call as soon as he woke up?

His hare dresser.

Which train takes you to the best Easter party in town?

Easter eggs-press.

Which is the Easter Bunny's favorite show?

The Kardashi-hens.

How do pigs show love and support to each other?

By holding each others hamds.

What is a jelly bean's favorite kind of music?

Beanie-weenie ballads.

What did the bunnies and eggs have in common?

They had no hambition in life.

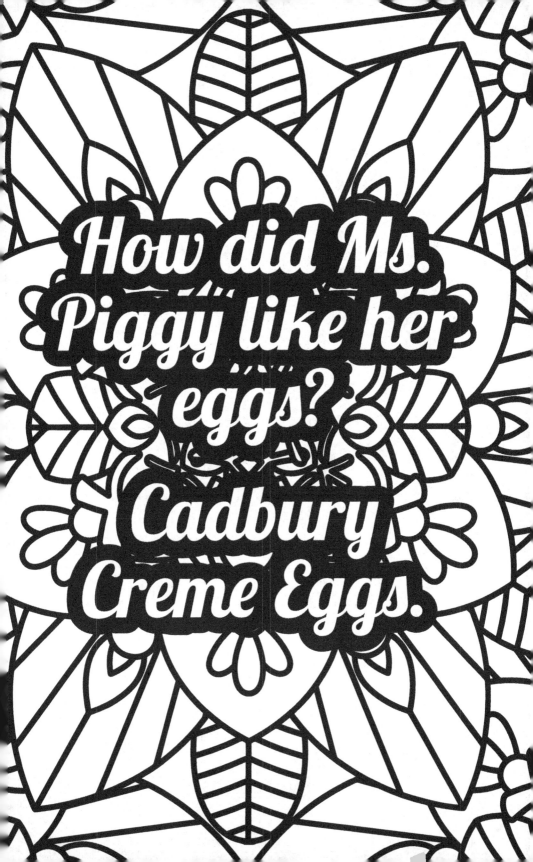

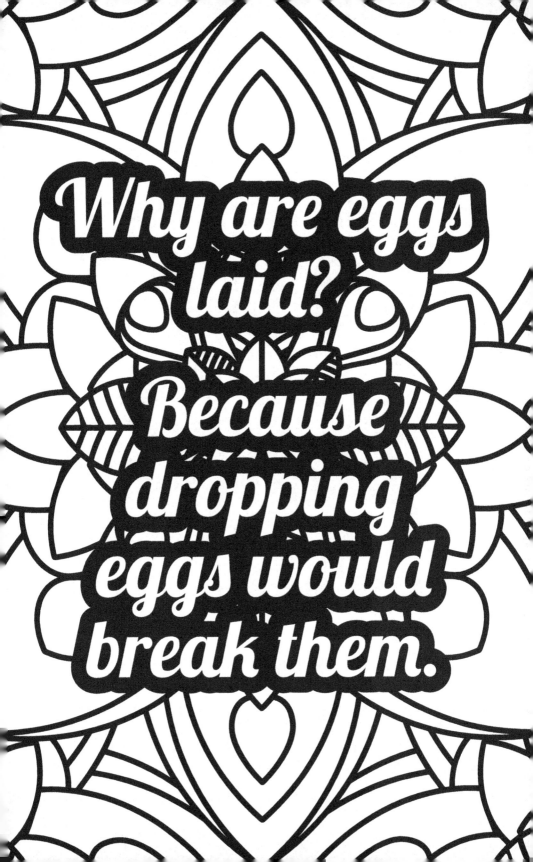

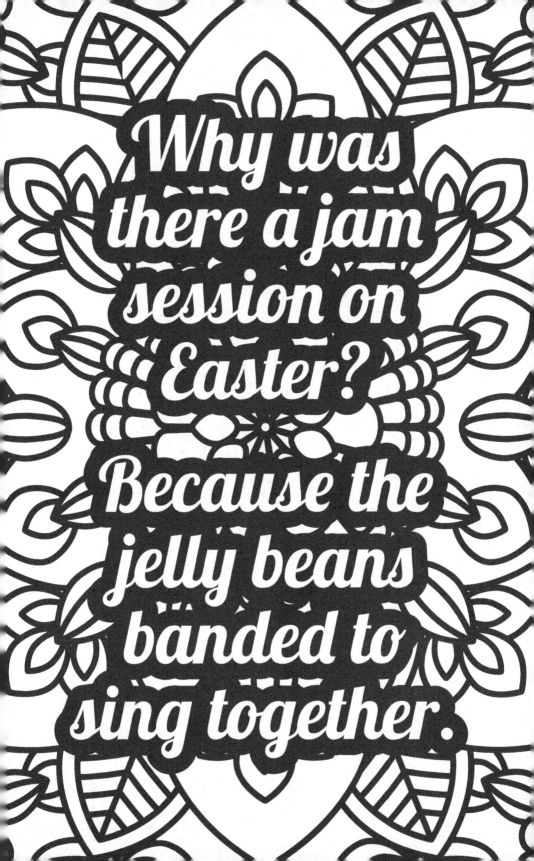

Why was there a jam session on Easter?

Because the jelly beans banded to sing together.

What were the angry potato's words during the fight?

You better be careful, or I'll mash you!

What do you call an Easter Bunny who loves his Easter eggs too much?

Easter egg-centric

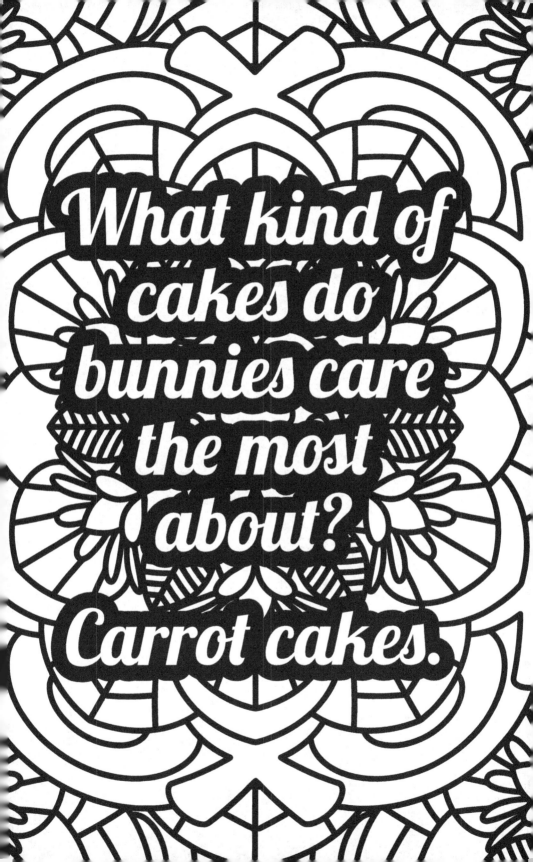

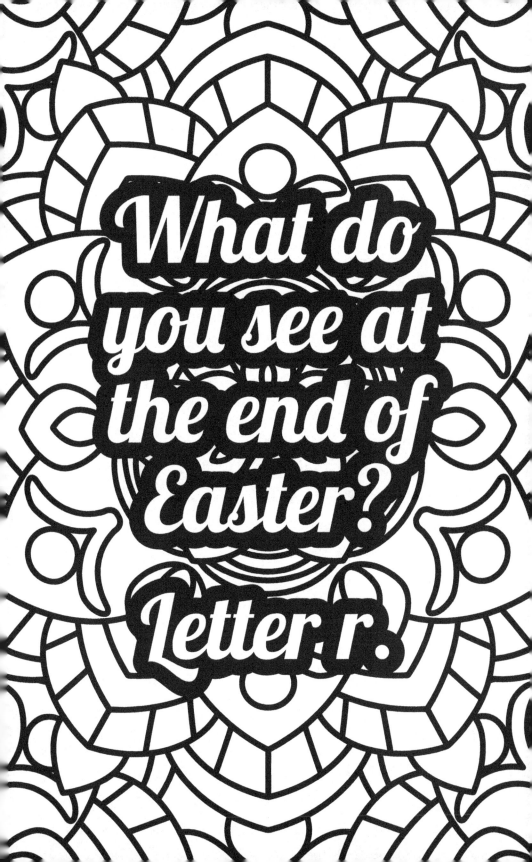

What do you see at the end of Easter?

Letter r.

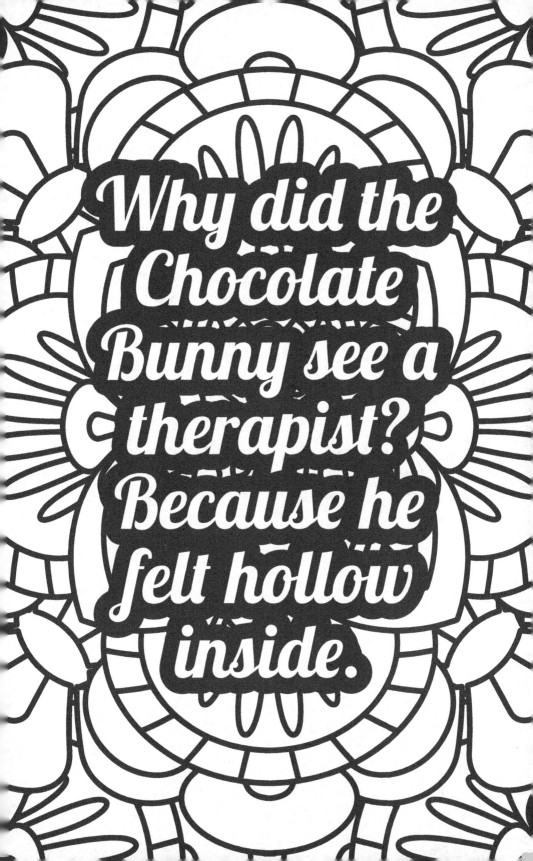

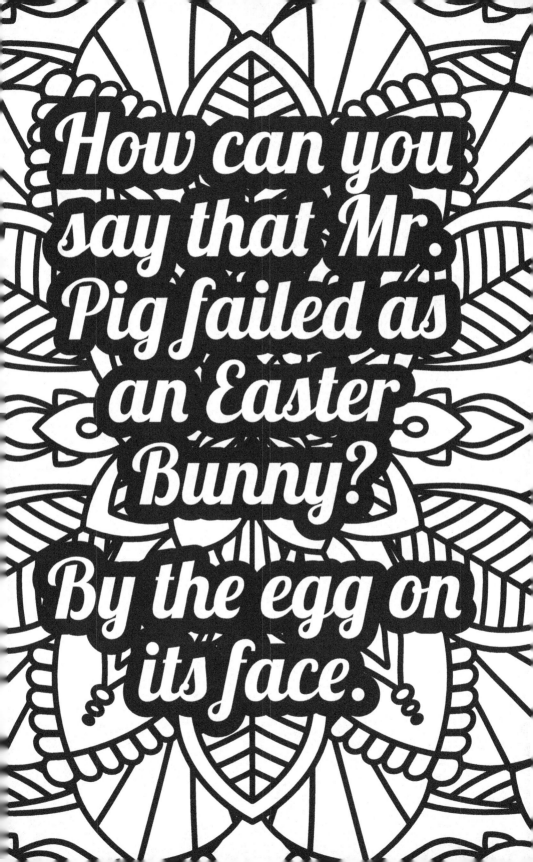

How can you say that Mr. Pig failed as an Easter Bunny?

By the egg on its face.

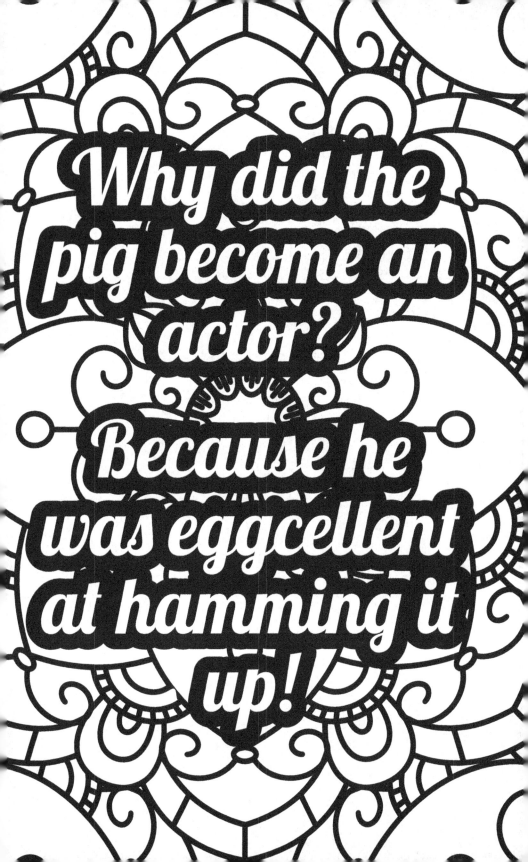

What did Mr. Pig say to Ms. Piggy when she was leaving angrily? I am bacon you to stay, please.

How did the Easter story book end?

All the characters lived HOPPILY ever after.

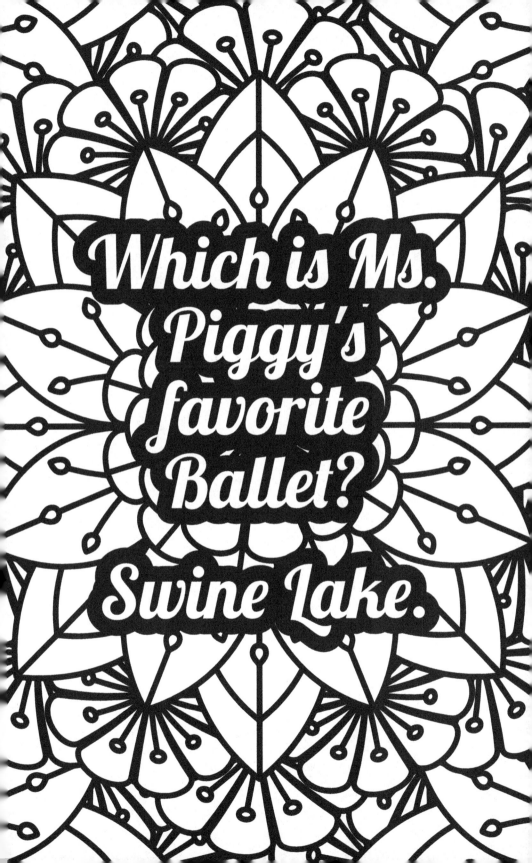

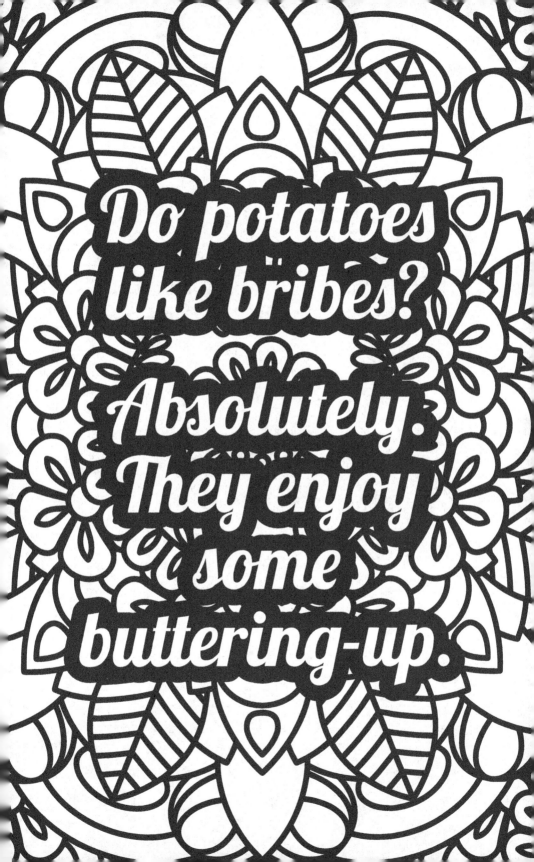

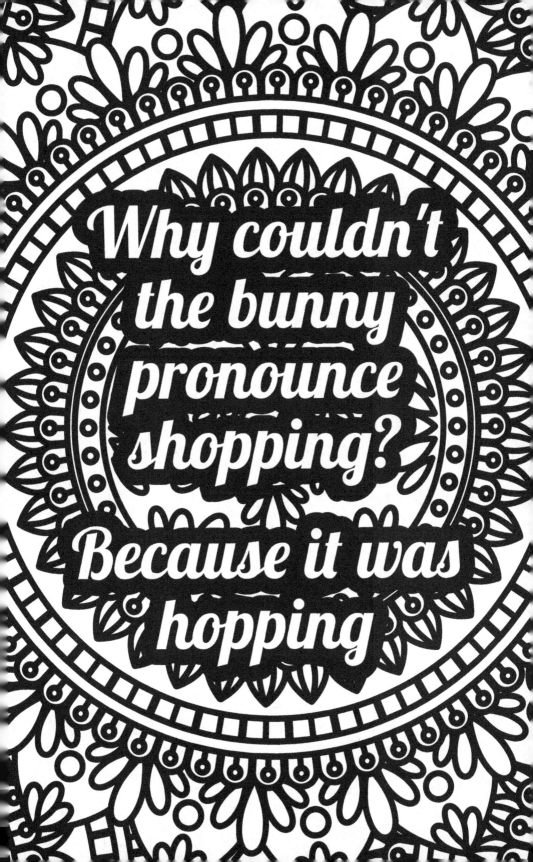

What is Bunny's aviation fleet called?

Hare Force

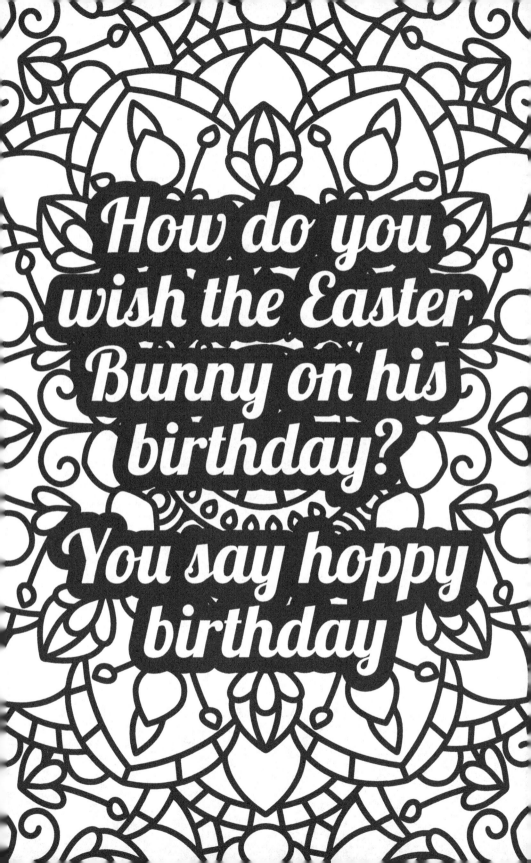

What do piglets listen to before going to sleep? Piggy tales.

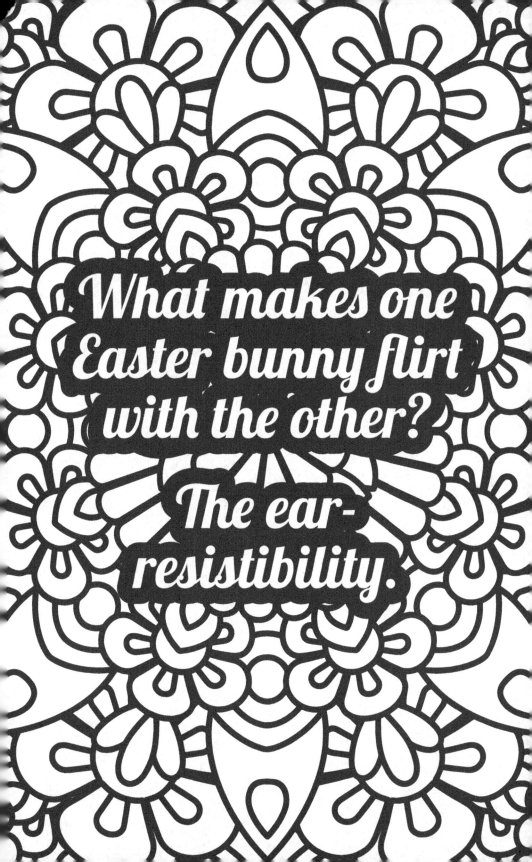

86013646R00059